Crazy Cat lady

This edition published in 2019

By SJG Publishing, HP22 6NF, UK

© Susanna Geoghegan Gift Publishing

Author: Michael Powell
Illustrator: Bryony Clarkson
Cover design: Milestone Creative
Contents design: Joanna Ross,
Double Fish Design Ltd

ISBN: 978-1-911517-80-1

Printed in China

10 9 8 7 6 5 4 3 2 1

Introduction

This book is unapologetically about crazy cat ladies, but even if that makes your hackles rise, please read on.

Right now, the world isn't demanding anything that lazily cashes in on the soft target trope of a crazy lady surrounded by felines. Who needs that? Or perhaps the opposite is true, as the demand for even a slim volume like this is probably miniscule – poking fun at crazy cat ladies – that one probably doesn't even exist in print, so clearly it's an answer without a question, a solution without a problem.

In short, it's a terrible idea – an entire book about crazy cat ladies – really? You've got to be kitten me! For starters, humour usually needs a high-status target that urgently needs taking down a peg or two. Crazy cat ladies are already a marginalised minority, so where's the sense in attacking them?

This book must attempt to go in to bat for those crazy ladies, otherwise it will simply rekindle old stereotypes and cause renewed harm. Cat ladies don't deserve to be kicked when they are down. If anything, they should be vigorously tickled to put a smile on their cranky faces, or be offered help with the vacuuming, because those cat hairs get literally everywhere.

DID YOU

Hear That?

If you're a sociopath and devoid of empathy, then you'll be disappointed to learn that you won't find any soft targets or cheap laughs in this book. For example, there won't be any jokes about lonely, eccentric fruitcakes who spend all day in their dressing gown and slippers, curtains drawn. Don't expect to find any easy quips like these:

Why are cats like potato chips?
You can never have just one.

Why did the cat lady run from the tree?
Because she was afraid of the bark.

What do cat ladies eat for breakfast?
Mice Krispies.

Why are cat ladies so grouchy?
Because they're in a bad mewd.

Instead, this book will highlight the plight of the crazy cat ladies among us, and celebrate this much maligned fringe of society. It will attempt to disrupt the persistent patriarchal impulse to discredit and attack women who fall outside cultural norms by pairing them with kitty cats. It will strive to challenge lazy stereotypes surrounding the issue whenever they crop up in the text. From now on. Starting ... now.

It's also an informative self-help guide that can help people and their families and friends to identify crazy cat ladylikeness. For example, there's a section on why your cat totally owns you, as well as self-care suggestions for stressed-out cat ladies, and advice on how to change your inner dialogue.

To some blind souls,
all cats are much
alike. To a cat lover,
every cat from the
beginning of time
has been utterly and
amazingly unique.

Jenny de Vries

If someone has gifted you this book, then you may already need urgent help.

Rest assured that as we share this journey, there will be plenty of opportunities to laugh *with* rather than *at* crazy old cat ladies, as well as to enjoy a healthy giggle at our own foibles. For example:

Did you hear about the cat lady who
swallowed a ball of wool?
She had mittens.

Now that's a great joke because it has internal logic, but it doesn't make cat ladylikeness the butt. Here's another one:

Why don't cat ladies play poker in the jungle?
Too many cheetahs.

That's right – cat ladies don't play poker in the jungle; many of them don't play poker at all or any of its variants, and cheetahs live in a variety of environments, including dry forests, grasslands, open plains and desert regions. So the joke is firmly grounded in reality, and also manages to be side-splittingly funny without recourse to lazy stereotypes.

CAT LADIES' HALL OF FAME: 1755–1793

Marie Antoinette

The ill-fated Austrian wife of France's King Louis XVI is notorious for remarking 'Let them eat cake' upon learning that the starving peasants of Paris had no bread, although there is no record of her having said it. Her love of small dogs is well known, but Versailles was also home to numerous cats. In fact, there were so many animals at the decadent royal palace that visitors sometimes remarked on its squalor, as Marie Antoinette allowed her six white Turkish Angora cats free rein during court functions.

On 16th October 1793, aged 37, Marie Antoinette was executed by guillotine in Paris after the Revolutionary Tribunal convicted her of high treason. According to legend, her beloved Angora cats were shipped from the port of Le Havre in France by Captain Samuel Clough, and were transported to Wiscasset in Maine, USA, where they interbred with the local population to produce the Maine Coon breed.

The way to get on with a cat is to treat it as an equal – or even better, as the superior it knows itself to be.

Elizabeth Peters

TEN REASONS WHY CATS ARE
Awesome

1) Humans and cats share about 90 per cent of their genetic code. This means that humans are mostly made out of cat, and vice versa.

2) Structurally, a cat's brain is also 90 per cent like a human brain – more similar than a dog's brain. No wonder cats and humans get along so well.

3) Only 3 per cent of a cat's brain is frontal lobes, compared to 25 per cent in humans. Consequently, cats are remorseless serial killers who can eat a whole tub of ice cream without getting brain freeze.

4) Humans and bananas also share about 60 per cent of their genetic code, which means humans are more than half banana. So every time a human eats a banana, they are more than half cannibal. Cats do not judge humans for this (mainly because of their frontal lobe deficiencies).

5) Numerous YouTube videos prove that cats are easily spooked by bananas, yet they bravely overcome their fear so that they can hang out with humans.

6) The average human consists of 65 per cent water. Cats are famously frightened of water, yet again they bravely overcome their fear so that they can hang out with humans.

7) Cats can sleep for as much as 16 hours a day, and older cats spend even more time being bone idle. Wild sloths sleep for about ten hours a day, yet they are widely considered to be the slowest and laziest mammals in the world. Cats are clearly very skilful at managing their public image. Sloths are rubbish by comparison.

8) Humans are shallower than cats. We love cats because of their cute furry little faces, but cats don't discriminate based on superficial physical characteristics such as cuteness or fur. A cat will happily curl up in the lap of the ugliest person in a room.

9) The Duke of Westminster, one of the richest men in Britain, allegedly inherited his father's £8.3bn fortune without paying a penny in death duties. Cats do not avoid tax.

10) Cats sweat through their paws, so their armpits smell fresh even when they forget to apply deodorant.

CAT LADIES' HALL OF FAME:
CHARLOTTE (1816–1855),
EMILY (1818–1848)
AND ANNE (1820–1849)

The Brontës

The Brontë sisters shared a love of writing and cats. Cats appear in many of their writings, including *Agnes Grey* and *Wuthering Heights*, as well as in their personal diaries. Emily even wrote a French essay in defence of cats, beguilingly entitled 'Le Chat' (The Cat). Household pets included the dogs Grasper, Keeper (a psycho mastiff) and Anne's beloved spaniel Flossy, a black tabby called Tom and another cat called Tiger. These animals kept the sisters company during their tragically short lives at the now famous parsonage, conveniently located next to the pay-and-display car park at the top of the West Yorkshire village of Howarth.

The problem with cats
is that they have the
exact same look on
their face whether
they see a moth
or an axe-murderer.

Paula Poundstone

EIGHT SIGNS THAT YOU ARE A CRAZY

Cat Lady

1) You have the cat shelter on speed dial.

2) One of the drawers in your bedroom is filled with tiny dressing-up clothes.

3) Strangers seeing your calves and forearms think you have been pruning too many rose bushes.

4) You need a new sofa, but spend the money on a deluxe twelve-story scratcher activity centre, lounger and hammock.

5) You delete family photos from your phone to make room for more cat pics.

6) Every birthday, you make your cats a huge cake out of tuna with peanut butter icing.

7) Every Christmas, your Secret Santa present is another copy of *Crafting with Cat Hair*.

8) You feel proud when people call you a crazy cat lady, but really you'd prefer to be a cat.

CAT LADIES' HALL OF FAME: 1921–1995

Patricia Highsmith

American novelist and short-story writer Patricia Highsmith was best known for writing *Strangers on a Train* and *The Talented Mr Ripley*. She wasn't a people person – one of her publishers, Otto Penzler, described her as a 'mean, cruel, hard, unlovable, unloving human being'. She was, however, heavily into cats, and as a friend surmised, she 'needed cats for psychological balance'.

She was always surrounded by her cats while she wrote, slept and – according to screenwriter Phyllis Nagy – subsisted on a diet of 'scotch, beer and cigarettes'. The heroes of her novels were 'deviants and genial psychopaths', so maybe she drew some inspiration for her characters from the feline world.

Cats can work out mathematically the exact place to sit that will cause the most inconvenience.

Pam Brown

I regard cats as one of the great joys in the world. I see them as a gift of the highest order.

Tricia McCagh

HOW DO YOU KNOW YOUR CAT

Loves You?

Cat haters say that cats are solipsistic beings that can't form emotional attachments, or that they just pretend to tolerate humans because they haven't yet learned how to open tins of tuna. Cat lovers know this isn't true, and that they have myriad subtle displays of affection in their own unique way. As 80s cat-loving (probably) synth-pop wizard Howard Jones observed, 'What is love anyway?' Let us count the ways:

1) Your cat hasn't killed you yet, which is the clearest sign that your relationship is running relatively smoothly. Rest assured, your cat isn't merely allowing you to live so long as a healthy stockpile of tuna remains in the kitchen cupboard. Your cat could feed itself quite happily without your help – on mice, birds, squirrels, the leftovers from your neighbour's recycling bin …

2) Sometimes he lets you have a lie-in, and doesn't slap you in the face with his paw until at least 6:15 a.m.

3) Your cat greets you at the door even though she doesn't have to. She could stay daydreaming on the back of the sofa and wait for you to come and find her, but she trots dutifully in to the hall and starts rubbing herself against your legs to mask the nasty outside smells you dragged in with you. This is the cat equivalent of forcefully removing your clothes, dousing them with petrol and making a bonfire on the front lawn, because she loves you.

4) He recognises the sound of your engine. Cats are experts at recognising engines, not only because they secretly play Gran Turismo on your PlayStation while you're out, but also because they have to judge traffic all the time for their survival. Whether they're urban cats crossing busy roads or country cats listening for lone speeding motorists, an experienced cat can differentiate between every car. Your engine is benign because, as far as your cat is concerned, you only ever manoeuvre it slowly in and out of your drive (except when you drive to the vet).

5) She follows you around. In fact, sometimes she won't leave you alone. She perches on your shoulders as you sit on the toilet or stares at you while you take a shower. This is a sign that she loves you, albeit in the same way those thirty random people you've never met follow you on Twitter – they're promoting themselves but they haven't realised that you're not following them back.

6) Cats avoid eye contact, except when they are really happy and comfortable with someone – then they will lock eyes and give you a long, slow blink. This says, 'I love you so much that I trust you won't stove my head in with a ball-peen hammer while my eyes are momentarily shut'. Cats live in an existential nightmare in which mortality lurks around every corner, so you can't blame them for framing affection in such cold-blooded terms. Take the compliment.

7) Meows. Apart from mother cats with kittens, cats do not meow to other cats, only to humans. Your cat uses an entire repertoire of mews to personally communicate with you.

8) He head-butts you. In cat land, a head-butt is not an attempt to break someone's nose or render them unconscious. Instead, it is a sign of affection we humans have named 'bunting' to make it sound less feral. When your cat bunts you, he scent marks your face and may also be asking for attention.

If a fish is the movement of water embodied, given shape, then a cat is a diagram and pattern of subtle air.

Doris Lessing

9) When your cat repeatedly thumps on a closed door or claws at the new carpet – she loves you. She just won't leave you alone, even when you are begging for some sweet isolation. Whoever said cats are low maintenance lied to try and re-home some kittens.

10) He kneads you rhythmically with his paws, in a vain attempt to make milk gush forth from your shirt. OK, this behaviour is not really love; it's self-gratification, akin to squeezing the last blob of toothpaste from the tube or smacking an upturned bottle of ketchup.

11) She brings you headless vermin because she knows how much humans love receiving gifts. Plus she reckons you could benefit from a little hunting practice, which is why she brings you live ones as well.

12) He trips you up. When you find yourself spread-eagled on the floor yet again with a suspected broken hip, take comfort that your cat only gets under your feet because he loves you and wants you to get down on his level so he can nibble your nose. Plus, he thinks you deserve a rest.

13) Remember, cats are passive-aggressive – they hate conflict, but they're not exactly experts at emotional honesty and open dialogue. So instead of talking problems through, they'll go to the toilet on your pillow and then make you feel like it's your fault. That's cats – it comes with the territory.

RE-APPROPRIATE THE
Slur

Use this book to discover whether or not you are a crazy cat lady, but also to re-appropriate the slur. For too long now, cats have been used as a furry stick with which to beat and poke fun at women who fall outside cultural norms – from the mysterious familiars of witches during the Middle Ages, to the satirical cartoons which depicted brave suffragettes as cats in order to trivialise and dismiss their fight for the vote.

Once I was gone for a month and I was just miserable, so I flew back from Florida for two hours just to be home and see my cats.

Paula Poundstone

I live alone with cats,
books, pictures,
fresh vegetables
to cook, the garden,
the hens to feed.

Jeanette Winterson

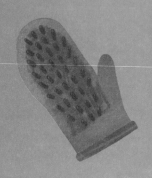

BASTET THE CAT
Goddess

The 'crazy cat lady' stereotype has been pervasive for so long that it's easy to forget that 5,000 years ago the Ancient Egyptians – the most sophisticated civilisation on the planet – worshipped Bastet, a cat goddess who was half cat half woman.

Bastet was revered as a good mother, so Egyptian women who wanted children sometimes wore an amulet of the goddess with kittens. This cat lady was a fertility symbol, a far cry from our modern, outdated associations.

In 450 BC, the Greek historian Herodotus visited Bastet's red granite temple at Bubastis, and described it as the most beautiful in the whole of Egypt. He estimated that 700,000 people made a pilgrimage there every year. Thousands of cats lived in the lush temple grounds, looked after by Bastet's priests, and those who could afford it sent their own dead cats to Bubastis to be embalmed and buried in vast underground cat cemeteries along the banks of the Nile. Not once did anyone dare suggest that these owners were crazier than a bag of frogs. Where did it all go wrong?

MUMMIFIED

Cats

More than 300,000 mummified cats were discovered when Bastet's temple was excavated. In 1888, Victorian archaeologists discovered a further 80,000 mummified cats and kittens at a site at Beni Hassan dated to 1000–2000 BC. An eyewitness account by William Martin Conway, the Baron of Allington (1856–1937), warned of the need to stand 'well windward' because the village children had plundered the site to find intact cat mummies to sell to tourists:

'The path became strewn with mummy cloth, and bits of cat skulls, bones and fur in horrid positions, and the wind blew the fragments about and carried the stink afar'.

Egyptian peasants had unwrapped thousands of mummies, looking for gold amulets. The discarded linen wrappings were later sold to the United States to make linen-based paper during the American Civil War, and about twenty tonnes of unwrapped cat mummies were shipped to Liverpool to be sold as fertilizer.

Dogs eat.

Cats dine.

Ann Taylor

Most cats are not shy about letting their people know what they want.

Karen Duprey

A SCATTERING OF MISPLACED

Faeces

Sharing your house with cats can understandably feel like the high security wing of a jail, surrounded by killers, psychopaths and general mayhem. The public perception is that cat ladies tend to put the cats' needs first, to the detriment of the state of the house. Cats can be very destructive animals, so torn upholstery, dubious stains and a scattering of misplaced faeces are strong indicators.

There is also a consensus within the neighbourhood that the cat lady is the go-to person when kittens urgently need re-homing.

On the whole, a cat lady is viewed sympathetically as a selfless individual who cares about the welfare of her animals. The 'crazy' prefix is subjectively added by society when the mental health of the individual has been tipped over the edge, often by too many cats and too little contact with the outside world.

TWENTY REASONS WHY CATS ARE BETTER THAN

Children

1) Cats just destroy your furniture; children ruin your entire life.

2) The ugliest kitten is cuter than the cutest baby.

3) Kittens learn to use a litter tray when they're about four weeks old; babies take a LOT longer.

4) A cat will never ask you what your favourite colour is.

5) You don't have to take your cat to a nice restaurant only to have them ruin it by being fussy eaters, making too much noise, hogging the conversation, running around between the tables and needing the toilet just as your food arrives.

6) Children are always falling over and crying. Cats don't even make much fuss after they've been run over.

7) Cats never demand a mobile phone. And if they had a phone, your cat would take good care of it, and wouldn't sit on it the very first day, cracking the screen.

8) A large cat could probably win a scrap with a badger; a baby wouldn't have a clue.

9) When cats have fights, they sort it out among themselves and you never have to get involved, except occasionally when they need stitches at the vet.

One reason that cats are happier than people is that they have no newspapers.

Gwendolyn Brooks

10) When you go to the cinema, you never have to watch a film made for cats, and pay a small fortune to stuff your cat with popcorn.

11) Cats don't bring home rubbish art and expect you to hang it on the fridge.

12) You don't have to send five-year-old cats off to school just to regain some sanity.

13) You don't have to pay for your cat's driving lessons.

14) When you go on holiday, you don't have to take your cats with you.

15) When you get divorced, your cat doesn't take sides.

16) You can legally get a cat high on catnip.

17) You can get drunk while your cats are wide awake.

18) Lazy cats are just like everyone else's cats; lazy kids are losers who make you look bad.

19) When your kids grow up and have children, they expect you to help look after them. You can get your cat spayed.

20) When your cat dies, you can bury it for free in the back garden.

SO WHAT IS A CRAZY

Cat Lady?

We know that crazy cat ladies come in all shapes, sizes, ages and flavours. You may even be one, which is why you bought this book (or more likely, someone bought it for you). Not all cat ladies are barking mad (barking like a dog, ironic); some are merely eccentric.

The first important order of business is to determine whether 'crazy cat lady' is a meme, cliché, stereotype or trope. (You can play along at home. Take a guess and then read on. You see? Already this book is turning out to be more highbrow and educational than the cover and title suggest.)

A meme is a bit of information, an element of a culture, an image, video, piece of text, etc. which is spread from person to person, often with slight variations (like a virus). A cliché is a word or phrase that has been over-used, and often betrays a lack of original thought. A stereotype is a widely-held but oversimplified idea of a particular type of person or thing. A trope is a significant or recurrent theme, or a figurative or metaphorical use of a word or expression. So ... 'crazy cat lady' is a trope, cliché and stereotype, but not really a meme. That said, if you google 'crazy cat lady memes,' you will find plenty. But those are memes that use 'crazy cat lady' as their theme; she isn't really a meme in and of herself.

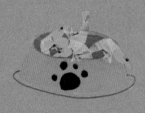

Take one female cat over a seven-year period. If all the kittens survived and bred, she would be responsible for 21,000 cats – they are such prolific breeders, you can see how important it is to neuter.

Celia Hammond

CAT LADIES' HALL OF FAME: 1821–1912

Clara Barton

The famous American nurse, teacher, vegetarian and founder of the Red Cross was crazy about all animals, but especially cats. During the Civil War, her selfless work earned her the nickname 'Angel of the battlefield', and inspired Senator Schuyler Colfax to send her a kitten with a bow around its neck. (Indeed, quite patronizing for one of the most important humanitarians of her generation!)

Clara's companion of seventeen years was her favourite cat, Tommy, who had black and white markings and green eyes. In 1885, Antoinette Margot painted a portrait of Tommy which still hangs in the Barton house in Glen Echo, Maryland, USA.

FIVE COOL YOUNG WOMEN WHO LOVE

Their Cats

You don't have to be old and crazy to be a crazy cat lady. These young movers and shakers prove that cat-loving can be cool.

1) Taylor Swift has two beloved Scottish fold cats – Meredith Grey (named after Ellen Pompeo's character from medical drama television series Grey's Anatomy) and Olivia Benson (named after Mariska Hargitay's character from Law & Order: Special Victims Unit). She appears to treat them like ordinary cats, except that they have personalised luggage.

2) Katy Perry has two cats, Monkey and Kitty Purry, who had a cameo in the video for Perry's breakout hit, 'I Kissed A Girl'. Perry also used a large inflatable Kitty Purry head on stage during her Hello Katy Tour.

3) Amanda Seyfried has two cats, Diane and Fran the elder, who appear frequently on her Instagram feed, along with a rescue dog named Finn. She and her husband also foster kittens from Best Friends Animal Society until they are old enough to be adopted.

4) Bella Thorne has nineteen cats – because she refused to neuter her first cat, Lola, so now she has four generations of cats living in a specially commissioned cat castle she had built for them in her home. Curiously, they rarely appear on her Instagram account.

5) Nicole Richie took in stray grey-striped alley cat, Tabitha Jones Madden, after it appeared on her doorstep: 'One dark and lonely night, I heard a little puss puss cry from outside. At first, I thought it was Joel. But to my surprise, there she was. A sad, and very hungry kitten.' Tabitha now lives la dolce vita in a tiny replica Italian villa with a framed photo of Nicole inside.

One is never sure when watching two cats washing each other whether it's affection, the taste or a trial run for the jugular.

Helen Thomson

A DAY IN THE LIFE OF A CRAZY

Cat Lady

05:26 woken by a cat batting face

05:35 woken again by two cats running around wearing jackboots pushing a wheelbarrow with square wheels (sounds like)

05:45 woken by headless squirrel on pillow

05:55 woken by cat hocking up fur ball

06:00 woken by alarm clock - hit snooze

06:03 woken by cat knocking alarm clock onto floor

06:30 woken by the feeling of being stared at by several cats, having overslept by twenty minutes (note: buy new alarm clock)

06:35 clean litter trays, feed cats, change water

06:55 shower

06:58 spend fifteen minutes applying salt wash to Cat #2 tooth abscess

07:13 spend ten minutes adding ear drops to Cat #1

07:23 get dressed

07:25 spend ten minutes brushing Cat #4 and applying eye drops

07:35 eat slice of toast, apply make up

07:36 check Facebook, spend four minutes watching video of cat riding around on a robot vacuum cleaner

07:40 remove cat faeces from the arm of the sofa, spray with kitchen cleaner (note: buy more pet stain and odour remover)

07:50 look for house key

08:00 find house key in fish bowl, search for fish

08:05 call off search for fish, leave house and run to bus stop, miss bus

09:14 arrive late at work, then work while talking (and worrying) about the cats

12:30 rush home during lunch break to apply salt wash, ear and eye drops

12:47 Cat #3 has climbed into an empty Jaffa Cakes box and looks cute, so spend ten minutes searching for your phone so you can take a pic, find underneath sleeping Cat #5, by which time Cat #3 has gone

12:57 spend six minutes searching for Cat #3, and another seven minutes trying to coax it back into the box

13:10 squash grumpy cat into Jaffa Cakes box and take lame photo, post to Facebook, eat sandwich, trip over cat and bash knee, feel faint, miss bus

14:14 arrive back at work, then work while talking about (and hating) most of the cats

17:25 get fired

What greater gift than the love of a cat?

Charles Dickens

17:30 leave work, buy pet stain and odour remover, knee compress bandage, cat treats, cat toys, eight cans of tuna and one tub of ice cream

18:25 arrive home, feed cats, change water, change litter trays, apply salt wash, ear and eye drops

19:16 eat ice cream, drink bottle of Zinfandel, slump on sofa crying, binge watch *Most Haunted* while acting as a cat mattress and toilet, fall asleep

22:18 wake up, remove cat faeces and goldfish tail from shoulder

22:30 go to bed, spend three hours being kept awake by five cats with prosthetic wooden legs dragging sacks of crockery up and down the stairs (sounds like)

01:30 fall asleep, dream about Golden Retrievers.

CAT LADIES' HALL OF FAME: 1913–1967

Vivien Leigh

Vivien Leigh was the most talented and beautiful actress of her time, who won two Academy Awards for Best Actress for her iconic performances as Scarlett O'Hara in *Gone with the Wind* and Blanche DuBois in A *Streetcar Named Desire*.

She was crazy about cats, and especially Siamese – 'Once you have kept a Siamese cat, you would never have any other kind. They make wonderful pets, and are so intelligent they follow you around like little dogs.'

Her cats travelled all over the world with her, including a black-and-white stray called Tissy, her first Siamese called New Boy (a gift from her husband Laurence Olivier, and named after a West End theatre), Armando and her favourite – a smoky white Siamese with black markings called Poo Jones (named after her favourite brand of Welsh laxatives!)

Who among us hasn't envied a cat's ability to ignore the cares of daily life and to relax completely?

Karen Brademeyer

After scolding one's cat,
one looks into its face
and is seized by the
ugly suspicion that it
understood every word.
And has filed it for
reference.

Charlotte Gray

WHY ARE WOMEN AND CATS SUCH

a Crazy Combination?

The 'cat lady' trope is the Western modern equivalent of the witch of medieval times. However back then, witches were associated with promiscuity and sinful lust, so the medieval witch was at the other end of the sexual activity spectrum to today's stereotype of a cat lady. This proves once again the hypocrisy that women are persecuted for being too sexually active *and* sexless.

TWENTY WAYS YOUR CAT TOTALLY

Owns You

1) As already discussed earlier, your cats could kill you while you sleep. They choose not to because they love you, or you because they are still waiting for the signal from the mothership. Now that's quite a considerable power imbalance in a relationship! If you're OK with that then that's your funeral, but one thing is clear – your cats own you.

2) Your life goes on pause whenever you see one of the cats doing something funny or cute, and so you have to take a photo with your phone.

3) Remember that angora jumper that you really liked which turned up on the floor of the airing cupboard because your pregnant cat was using it for a nest and you couldn't bear to take it away from her so you wrote it off as an early kitty shower present? Ownage.

4) You spend two hours looking for the TV remote control, then the cat fixes your gaze, jumps off the sofa and there's the remote, right underneath her.

5) Cats demand absolute privacy when they go to the toilet, and if you dare put the litter tray in the wrong place, they will go just next to it, until you move the tray one inch into the perfect position. But when you're using the toilet, you become the number one attraction.

6) It has been estimated that around 3 million cats are eaten every year. You'd never eat one though, because you are owned.

7) You know when your cat flashes her belly at you and lies enticingly on the floor, tempting you to give her a gentle tummy rub, and she enjoys the first three seconds then turns psycho without warning? That's called gaslighting.

It is impossible to keep a straight face in the presence of one or more kittens.

Cynthia E Varnado

8) Your cat loves freaking you out by staring intently at nothing, so you start imagining that either there's a giant spider that you can't see, or maybe the ghost of a dead relative is hovering behind your shoulder. And he always seems to do it when you're on your own watching something scary on the television. More gaslighting.

9) A cat will often greet you by turning away, lifting his tail and showing his bottom. Rude.

10) You have a long, relaxing petting session with your favourite feline, and she appears to enjoy it too, nuzzling into your hands and purring deeply. Then suddenly, she jumps onto the floor and spends the next hour obsessively licking to remove all traces of filthy human. You feel gutted.

11) Your cat will attack your ankles if she's under stimulated. You get painful scratches and even bite marks on your feet, and you blame yourself for not playing with her enough. In what other scenario could you get violently ambushed and think it's your fault? You're totally under her control.

12) She steals your socks. Your socks.

13) If you suspect that your cats ignore you most of the time, you'd be right. Recent research shows that on average, cats choose to respond to their names being called once in every ten times.

14) Cats have a special high-pitched 'cry' which they use to manipulate humans because it sounds like a human baby, to which we are hard wired to respond. Yeah, that's right – cats impersonate our children in distress to get what they want.

15) At some time in our lives, every one of us has felt personally victimised by a cat.

16) He leaves decapitated animals on your pillow.

17) Cats do their business in a box – which YOU empty.

18) Cats can rotate their ears 180 degrees. But sometimes they don't even bother to move their ears when you call their name. Rude.

19) Your nine-year-old cat sleeps so much that she has only been awake for three years of her life.

20) Cats can drink seawater. If you were stranded in a boat at sea with a cat, it could survive by drinking seawater, but you'd have to survive by drinking cat wee. Owned.

A cat can purr its way out of anything.

Donna McCrohan

THE MALLEUS

Maleficarum

The medieval persecution of witches can be traced back to one man – a discredited Dominican friar called Heinrich Kramer who loved nothing better than conducting inquisitions until the religious establishment banned him from torturing cat ladies. However, this didn't stop him from publishing in 1487 his famous treatise on witchcraft, *The Malleus Maleficarum*, the very title of which betrays Heinrich's violent preoccupations – it translates as Hammer of Witches.

Despite its condemnation by the Inquisition, *The Malleus Maleficarum* cemented in the gullible public consciousness the idea of cats as familiars, and that witches turned into cats at night. And so, a demented, discredited misogynistic treatise written by a sadistic clergyman became the driving force for the persecution of cat-loving ladies in secular courts throughout Renaissance Europe, and for decades to come.

CAT LADIES' HALL OF FAME: 1832–1888

Louisa May Alcott

American novelist, poet, abolitionist, feminist and suffragette best known as the author of the semi-autobiographical novel *Little Women*, Louisa May Alcott had an 'inordinate love of cats' by her own admission. After a poverty-stricken rural upbringing and working as a teacher and seamstress to support her family, she was treated with toxic levels of mercury after contracting typhoid fever while briefly nursing at Washington, D.C. during the US Civil War. She spent the rest of her adult life suffering from a weakened immune system, vertigo and episodes of hallucinations.

ARE YOU UNLUCKY

In Love?

Don't despair. Cats are much better companions than humans, especially men. They are totemic and talismanic. In nearly all of the greatest tragic love stories, the woman would fare better if she had taken in a few stray cats instead of losing her mind over a man.

In Shakespeare's tragedy of doomed young love, if a cat rather than hot-headed Romeo had discovered Juliet insensible, it may have pawed her face a few times and nibbled her nose, but there's no way it would have hastily chugged a vial of poison. Juliet would have woken up, seen the cat was fine and lived happily ever after.

In *An Affair to Remember*, Deborah Kerr could have retained the use of her legs if she had stayed at home with a clowder of cats, instead of getting run over while hurrying to a rendezvous with Cary Grant at the top of the Empire State Building, therefore saving lots of romantic kerfuffle.

If Anna Karenina had taken in a few strays instead of embarking on an extra-marital affair with the dashing cavalry officer Count Alexei Kirillovich Vronsky, Leo Tolstoy could have put a bit more effort into his own doomed marriage and the world could have been spared eight hundred turgid pages about gender, social class, railways and the Russian feudal system.

If Catherine Earnshaw had been merely hissed at (or more likely, ignored) by a cat while spying at Thrushcross Grange, she could have run home to Wuthering Heights and into the arms of Heathcliff instead of being trapped there for five weeks recuperating from a dirty dog bite.

And of course, two generations of heartache could have been avoided if Miss Haversham had bred Exotic Shorthairs instead of raising an orphaned baby to break men's hearts.

If your cat falls out of a tree, go indoors to laugh.

Patricia Hitchcock

SOCIAL PATTERNED
Defect

What is so inexplicably curious is why the 'crazy cat lady' becomes so maligned, shunned by society and a figure of ridicule at the moment of her greatest vulnerability – when she most needs it, she actually loses her humanity by being reduced to a trope. Surely that's the sign of a sick society rather than a sick individual? Millions of supposedly sane people share the same mental pathology – that cat ladies are crazy, and the crazier they are, the more they should be ridiculed.

This phenomenon is what the famous German social psychologist, psychoanalyst and humanistic philosopher Eric Fromm called social patterned defect: 'A pathogenic belief system that becomes normative and sets the stage for behaviours … among the majority that impair our capacity for reason and love, but receive such intense and widespread social validation that they do not give rise to inner conflict.' In short, it's why society pokes fun at ladies who keep sixteen multipacks of tuna in otherwise bare kitchen cupboards.

WHAT ARE THE DEFINING FEATURES OF

a Cat Lady?

In a recent study by Carroll University in Wisconsin, psychologists found that cat lovers were on average more educated, and scored higher on intelligence tests than those who preferred dogs or no animals at all. They also found cat people to be less conformist.

You don't have to be an old spinster to be a cat lady but you do have to share your home with a greater-than-normal number of cats. Only you can judge this.

Traditionally, there is an association with cat ladies being unlucky in love and living alone, thereby enabling the time and the space to house local strays and hoard cats. However, the hall of fame cat ladies demonstrate that you can lead an extraordinarily full life and still be crazy about cats.

Researchers from the University of Texas in Austin

recently questioned 4,500 people about their preference for cats and dogs, and found that cat people tended to be more introverted, sensitive and home-loving, while dog lovers described themselves as more extroverted and sociable. However, cat people were more open to new experiences. There are plenty of cool and successful young women today who love their cats.

I found out why cats drink out of the toilet. My mother told me it's because the water is cold in there. And I'm like: How did my mother know that?

Wendy Liebman

FROM PROMISCUOUS WITCH TO

Old Maid

The Victorians made the switch in perception of cat ladies from promiscuous witch to old maid. They retained the negative association between cats and women, but turned up the volume on the 'single woman without children' aspect. 'Old maids and cats have long been proverbially associated together, and rightly or wrongly, these creatures have been looked upon with a certain degree of suspicion and aversion by a large proportion of the human race,' wrote a journalist in the *Dundee Courier* in 1880. In the Victorian card game Old Maid, the Old Maid was depicted as an old woman with a cat.

CAT LADIES' HALL OF FAME: 1820–1910

Florence Nightingale

Florence Nightingale was an English social reformer and statistician credited with being the founder of modern nursing. She was also devoted to her cats. She owned more than 60 in her lifetime, and had as many as 17 at once. She rose to prominence during the Crimean War when she organised care for wounded soldiers and made huge strides in hospital hygiene and sanitation.

She prepared special food which she served to her cats on china plates. Her favourite was a large Persian named Mr Bismarck, 'the most sensitively affectionate of cats, very

gentle ... who never makes a mistake.' The
Crimean War destroyed her health (she
probably contracted chronic brucellosis
from drinking infected milk) and
she spent the next 52 years an
invalid writing countless papers,
pamphlets and books, surrounded by
her cats.

During the last two decades of her
life, she never left her second-storey
bedroom until her death, aged 90
when she was blind and senile. Tiny
inky paw prints can still be spotted
on several of her manuscripts,
which form part of one of the largest
collections of writings in the British Library.

It always gives me
a shiver when I see a
cat seeing what
I can't see.

Eleanor Farjeon

HOW TO REFUSE THE NEXT BOX OF

Homeless Kittens

Most cat ladies know that their lives are out of control, but their good nature and pride prevent them from admitting that they need help. Everyone knows that she who lives in that spooky house with the overgrown garden and broken fence will always take in another box full of kittens. She has a big heart but lacks assertiveness. She must learn to say no and put her own needs first for a change. The next time someone offers you a box of kittens, here are some strategies for saying no.

1) The multi-billionaire investor Warren Buffett said, 'The difference between successful people and very successful people is that very successful people say no to almost everything'. So say no, be assertive and courteous, but leave them in no doubt that 'no' means 'no' – don't given them even a chink of a possibility that you will cave in at the last minute and take the kittens off their hands.

2) Be firm. If someone can't accept your no, pretend to strangle a kitten in front of them (keep an old fluffy sock up your sleeve), and say you will do this every time they fail to listen to what you are saying.

3) Say: 'That's such an honour, and I feel privileged to have been asked. However, the truth is that I don't really like cats much. Yeah, I can see that maybe I send out mixed messages but nah, can't stand them. I'm more of a dog person. Thanks anyway. Bye now.'

4) Don't apologise and give lots of excuses, although research has shown that simply using the word

I have a cat, the pet that ranks just above a throw pillow in terms of required responsibility.

Anna Quindlen

A cat's name may tell you more about its owners than it does about the cat.

Linda W Lewis

'because' makes people agree with you even if your reason is transparently weak. Train operating companies use the same technique when announcing a delay: 'The ten-fifteen to … because of leaves on the line'. Any reason is better than keeping people in the dark.

5) Start juggling with three of the kittens while thanking the do-gooders. Explain that, unfortunately, your new hobby means you have to tolerate a lot of injured kittens, but you're improving every day.

6) Provide an alternative – place an equal number of your cats into another box and exchange it for the kittens.

7) Remember that your self-worth does not depend on pleasing other people, and that pleasing is nearly always a symptom of a deeper issue. If you have self-worth issues, they won't improve with another box of tiny mouths to feed. Pleasing others is never a route to happiness. Improving your self-worth begins with how you talk to yourself, how you change your inner dialogue.

CAT LADIES' HALL OF FAME

Honorary Mentions

Men shouldn't really be allowed too much space in a book about cat ladies, but these four creative dudes were such conspicuous cat lovers that they deserve a brief mention in dispatches.

AWESOME CAT DUDE: 1642–1727

Sir Isaac Newton

One of the most brilliant scientific minds of all time, Isaac Newton had few friends outside of his beloved cats (and dogs). However although he enjoyed their company, he is credited with inventing the cat flap so that he could work without disturbance. He cut two holes in the door of his study – a large one for the mother cat and a smaller one for her kittens.

AWESOME CAT DUDE: 1881–1973

Pablo Picasso

The genius Spanish painter, sculptor and co-founder of the Cubist movement was a sucker for cats. He shared his life with many cats, and they appeared frequently in his paintings. In 2006, his canvas called Dora Maar au Chat (Dora Maar with Cat) – which depicts his lover (French photographer, painter and poet Dora Maar) sitting in a chair with a small black kitten perched on her shoulder – sold at Sotheby's in New York for $95,216,000!

Samuel Langhorne Clemens

Better known by the pseudonym, Mark Twain, the famous American novelist, humourist, author of *The Adventures of Tom Sawyer* and *The Adventures of Huckleberry Finn* was an all-round good guy, an abolitionist and supporter of women's suffrage. He also loved cats, had lots of them and gave them complicated names such as Sour Mash, Apollinaris, Zoroaster, and Blatherskite 'to practice the children in large and difficult styles of pronunciation'. He so respected them that he refused to play pool if one of the cats was sleeping on the table.

He was in awe of a cat's indomitable spirit: 'A cat ain't ever anybody's slave or serf or servant, and can't be – it ain't in him to be. And so, he don't have to obey anybody. He is the only creature in heaven or earth or anywhere that don't have to obey somebody or other, including the angels ... there's always somebody a king has to obey ... but it ain't so with a cat.'

AWESOME CAT DUDE: 1802–1885

Victor Hugo

The French Romantic writer, poet and dramatist whose works include *Les Misérables* and *The Hunchback of Notre Dame* was a huge cat lover, who frequently gushed about his fondness for felines in his diary: 'God made the cat so that man might have the pleasure of caressing the tiger' and 'What is the cat? … it is a corrective. God, having made the mouse, said, 'I've made a blunder.' And he made the cat. The cat is the erratum of the mouse. The mouse, plus the cat, is the revised and corrected proof of creation.'

FIFTEEN MORE REASONS WHY CATS ARE

Better than Children

1) You don't have to battle with a cat to get it to wash its hands before a meal because it's already cleaned its entire body, twice!

2) Cats don't ask you how kittens are made.

3) When cats are happy, they calm you down by purring; when children are happy, they ruin everyone's life screaming, shouting and laughing.

4) When children are ill, you're supposed to stay up all night, fetching them medicine and keeping

their temperature down with a damp face cloth,
emptying buckets and talking with a soothing voice.
When your cat gets ill, it drags itself over to your
neighbour's shed.

5) When a child drops an ice cream on the floor, you
have to buy it another one immediately to stop it
screaming; a cat either licks it off the floor or walks
calmly away.

6) When your third child arrives, you have to buy a
bigger house and car.

7) When they eat, cats don't
smear food all over their faces
and on every other surface
they can reach. Children are
sticky, all the time, even
when they're not eating.

8) Both cats and young
children lack the
language skills to express
their emotions effectively,
but only children use this as
an excuse to throw massive
tantrums.

You own a dog but you feed a cat.

Jenny de Vries

9) You don't have to read to kittens to help them sleep.

10) A cat won't get strawberry jam on your iPad.

11) You can get in a lot of trouble if you refer to a baby as 'it'.

12) Unless you own a circus, you won't have to teach your cat to swim, read, count or ride a bike.

13) Most cats are OK with children; most children ARE NOT OK with cats.

14) Cats lower your blood pressure and reduce your risk of dying from a heart attack.

15) If your cat looks like Hitler, you can get rich by posting videos of it on YouTube, and people think you and your cat are awesome.

THE CAT AND
Mouse Act

Cats were also a common symbol in suffragette imagery. Anti-suffrage postcards depicted cats dressed up to look like female activists – figures of ridicule, because cats were domestic animals that were best suited to remaining at home, rather than fighting for equality. Ironically, this association came back to bite critics of women's suffrage, as hunger-striking suffragettes were treated horrifically in prison with force feeding, and they often sustained permanent injuries. When the government introduced a cynical act that allowed suffragettes to return home to recuperate before being rearrested when they were well, their ploy quickly became known as the Cat and Mouse Act.

I like cats. I used to have a lot of cats, but I don't anymore. Now I just have a dog. It does take a certain temperament to have a cat, as they do have certain personalities.

Jennifer Love Hewitt

The cat is above all things, a dramatist.

Margaret Benson

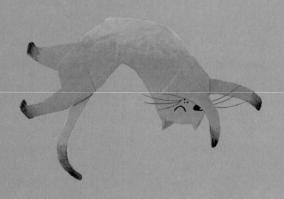

TEN SELF-CARE IDEAS FOR STRESSED-OUT

Cat Ladies

The key to getting out of that stressed cat lady rut is to make self-care a daily habit through your actions as well as your thoughts. It has nothing at all to do with treating yourself to a bath bomb or having a disappointing homemade face mask. Here are ten realistic self-care ideas to boost your self-esteem and make it second nature to put yourself first.

1) Let go of purrfectionism. It's hard to be happy when you set your personal standards impossibly high. Therefore don't try so hard. It's OK to spend your day slobbing around the house in your dressing gown and not brushing your hair all weekend ... oh, you already do? Um, well, way to go.

2) Reassess your priorities. When you race around trying to do everything, you end up doing nothing. So take some time to figure out what really matters. For example, which is more important – emptying

twelve cat litter trays three times a day or lying under a duvet crying? Actually, it's a trick question because you can do both.

3) Improve your diet. How can you expect to find the energy for a busy day looking after cats if you don't use top-quality fuel? Just making one small change to your diet can dramatically improve your energy levels – sorting your own breakfast before the cats' breakfasts will help maintain a healthy appetite.

4) Make time for exercise. You need to get out of breath for at least twenty minutes each day. Shaking a clingy cat off your pyjama leg every ten minutes; bending down to pick up cat toys and breathing into a paper bag to calm your panic attacks do not count.

5) Dial back your expectations of others. People sometimes suck the life out of you, and mostly you can't change them.

When you hold on to unrealistic expectations about other people, the only person who gets hurt is you. That said, don't be afraid to ask a friend for support. It always feels better to share an emotional burden with someone else than to keep it all inside.

6) Sit down and relax as you listen to Tom Hardy read a bedtime story.

7) Buy an adult colouring book and enjoy colouring in as you chill out wearing a fluffy onesie.

8) When grocery shopping, avoid buying food that you don't know how to cook or eat (e.g. chicory, tofu, Jerusalem artichoke, etc). It looks exciting at the farmers market, but when you take it home, it loses its magic every time you open the fridge door, slowly rotting and begging to be thrown away. If you can't even take care of the vegetables in your fridge, what are you doing with so many cats? You don't have time to learn pretentious new recipes. Save your money for a Friday night takeaway.

9) Put last week's dishes away (wash them first).

10) Write a cryptic attention-seeking post on social media, then sit back and wait for your concerned friends to tell you how loved and wonderful you are.

Time spent with a cat is never wasted.

Colette

CHANGE YOUR INNER DIALOGUE,

Think Like a Cat

Be more cat. Borrow your inner dialogue from what cats tell themselves, and keep repeating until you own it. It will boost your self-image, and help you love yourself again. Here are twenty positive 'catfirmations':

1) 'My coat is extra smooth and glossy this morning; I have the best tongue.'

2) 'I'm an excellent jumper.'

3) 'I have the power to destroy this cushion.'

4) 'I am in charge of how I feel, and today I am choosing lazy.'

5) 'I surround myself with peaceful people.'

6) 'I find joy and pleasure in the simplest things in life – like killing this feather.'

7) 'I love tuna.'

8) 'Yawn. Hmm … I think I'll just lie on this radiator for another couple of hours.'

9) 'Chatter chatter … bird … chatter … nyi-nyi-nyi-nyi-nyi-nyi-nyi-nyi.'

10) 'I want to sprint randomly while screaming, but it's not 3 a.m.'

11) 'By allowing myself to eat this mouse, I inspire others to eat mice as well.'

12) 'I attract treats easily into my life.'

13) 'My personality exudes confidence. I am bold and outgoing, but I hate cucumbers.'

14) 'If anyone touches my tummy today, I will bite them.'

15) 'Today, I shall mainly chew this woollen blanket.'

16) 'I love to nap on top of the bathroom cabinet.'

17) 'I am a creative force of nature, so sometimes I poo outside the tray.'

18) 'My life is joyously balanced as I sit motionless in this box.'

19) 'My potential to drink from the toilet is limitless.'

20) 'My life is abundant and full of fish-flavoured kibble.'

If cats could talk,
they wouldn't.

Nan Porter

You cannot look at
a sleeping cat and
feel tense.

Jane Pauley

TWELVE THINGS YOU'LL NEVER HAVE TO

Say to Your Cat

1) 'When I was your age …'

2) 'Eat your dinner first …'

3) 'Because I said so …'

4) 'Have you done your homework?'

5) 'Tidy your room.'

6) 'Hurry up and get ready …'

7) 'We're all waiting for you.'

8) 'Eat your vegetables.'

9) 'Are you sure you don't need a wee before we go out?'

10) 'Not while you're under my roof, you won't.'

11) 'We'll see …'

12) 'Why can't you be more like …?'

CAT LADIES' HALL OF FAME

The Cat Ladies of Rome

There are estimated to be 300,000 feral cats in Rome. In 1991 the cats living in the Coliseum, the Forum and Torre Argentina were declared part of Rome's 'bio-cultural heritage'.

In the centre of the city, a tiny cave-like space among the ruins at Torre Argentina serves as a cat sanctuary where a small army of mostly female volunteers – the Cat Ladies of Rome – take in strays, sterilise them and give them food and medicine. Twenty years ago, it was an abandoned shell with no electricity or running water, but the volunteers and the Anglo Italian Society for the Protection of Animals (AISPA) transformed it into a clean, modern facility with tiled floors, air conditioning and cages.

The refuge, which attracts tens of thousands of tourists a year, performs a vital service.